Nativity

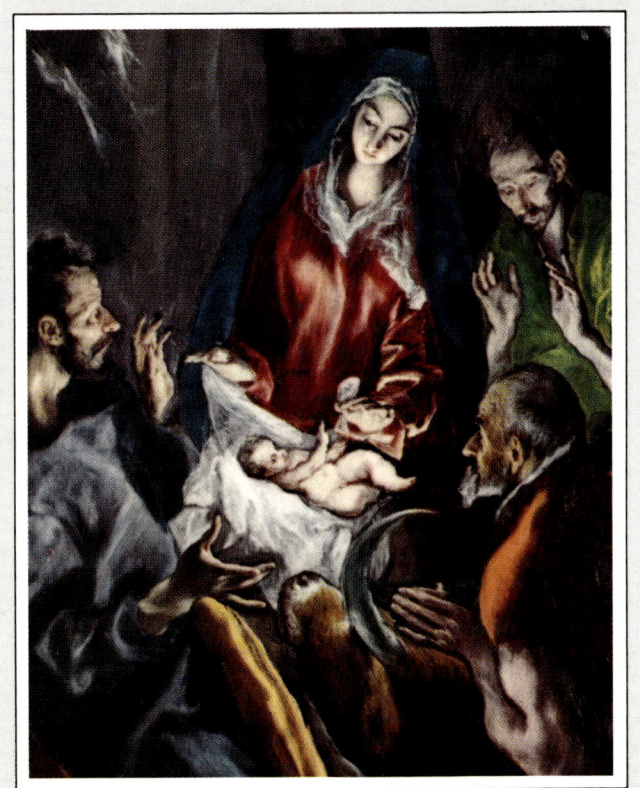

Nativity

Winston Press

Extracts from the Authorized King James
Version of the Bible, which is Crown
Copyright in England, are reproduced by
permission of Eyre & Spottiswoode, Her
Majesty's Printers.

Fra Angelico (1387-1455)
The Annunciation (detail)
Prado, Madrid

© 1983 Orbis Publishing Limited, London
This edition published by Winston Press, Inc.
All rights reserved.
Library of Congress Catalog Card Number: 82-62862
ISBN: 0-86683-726-4
Printed in Italy

Winston Press, Inc.
430 Oak Grove
Minneapolis, MN 55403

Front cover: Giovanni Battista Pittoni (1687-1767)
The Nativity with God the Father and the Holy Ghost
National Gallery, London

Half title: El Greco (1541-1614)
The Adoration of the Shepherds (detail)
Prado, Madrid

Frontispiece: Peter Paul Rubens (1577-1640)
The Adoration of the Magi (detail)
Musées Royaux des Beaux-Arts de Belgique, Brussels

Contents

The Annunciation 6

The Visitation 18

The Nativity 24

The Worship of the Shepherds 36

The Worship of the Magi 44

The Presentation 50

The Flight into Egypt 58

The Annunciation

AND in the sixth month the angel Gabriel was sent from God unto a city of Galilee, named Nazareth,
LUKE 1·26

Leonardo da Vinci (1452-1519)
The Annunciation (detail)
Uffizi, Florence

T O A virgin espoused to a man whose name was Joseph, of the house of David; and the virgin's name was Mary.

LUKE 1·27

Simone Martini (c. 1284-1344)
The Annunciation (detail)
Uffizi, Florence

Rogier van der Weyden (1399-1464)
The Annunciation (detail)
Louvre, Paris

AND the angel came in unto her, and said, Hail, thou that art highly favoured, the Lord is with thee: blessed art thou among women.

LUKE 1·28

AND when she saw him, she was troubled at his saying, and cast in her mind what manner of salutation this should be.

LUKE 1·29

Fra Filippo Lippi (c. 1406-69)
The Annunciation
National Gallery, London

AND the angel said unto her, Fear not, Mary: for thou hast found favour with God.

LUKE 1·30

AND, behold, thou shalt conceive in thy womb, and bring forth a son, and shalt call his name JESUS.

He shall be great, and shall be called the Son of the Highest: and the Lord God shall give unto him the throne of his father David:

LUKE 1·31-32

Sebastiano Mazzoni (1611-78)
The Annunciation
Gallerie Dell'Accademia, Venice

AND Mary said, Behold the handmaid of the Lord; be it unto me according to thy word.
LUKE 1·38

Giambattista Pittoni (1687-1767)
The Annunciation (detail)
Gallerie Dell'Accademia, Venice

The Visitation

Maestro della Vita di Maria (active c. 1450-90)
The Visitation
Alte Pinakothek, Munich

AND it came to pass, that, when Elisabeth heard the salutation of Mary, the babe leaped in her womb; and Elisabeth was filled with the Holy Ghost:

LUKE 1·41

AND she spake out with a loud voice, and said, Blessed art thou among women, and blessed is the fruit of thy womb.

LUKE 1·42

Raphael (1483-1520)
The Visitation
Prado, Madrid

AND Mary said, My soul doth magnify the Lord,

    And my spirit hath rejoiced in God my Saviour.

    For he hath regarded the low estate of his handmaiden: for, behold, from henceforth all generations shall call me blessed.

LUKE 1·46-48

AND Mary abode with her about three months, and returned to her own house.

LUKE 1·56

Piero di Cosimo (c. 1462-1521)
The Visitation with Saint Nicholas and Saint Anthony Abbot
National Gallery, Washington

The Nativity

BUT thou, Beth-lehem Ephratah, though thou be little among the thousands of Judah, yet out of thee shall he come forth unto me that is to be ruler in Israel;

MICAH 5·2

School of Amiens (French, c. 1437)
The Expectant Madonna with Saint Joseph
National Gallery, Washington

AND Joseph also went up from Galilee, out of the city of Nazareth, into Judaea, unto the city of David, which is called Bethlehem;

To be taxed with Mary his espoused wife, being great with child.

LUKE 2·4-5

Pieter Bruegel the Elder (c. 1525-69)
The Census in Bethlehem (detail)
Musées Royaux des Beaux-Arts de Belgique, Brussels

AND so it was, that, while they were there, the days were accomplished that she should be delivered.

And she brought forth her first-born son, and wrapped him in swaddling clothes, and laid him in a manger; because there was no room for them in the inn.

LUKE 2·6-7

Piero della Francesca (c. 1410/20-92)
The Nativity
National Gallery, Washington

AND the Word was made flesh, and dwelt among us, (and we beheld his glory, the glory as of the only begotten of the Father,) full of grace and truth.

JOHN 1·14

Gerrit van Honthorst (1590-1656)
The Nativity
Uffizi, Florence

Bartolomeo Vivarini (c.1432-c.1499)
The Nativity (detail)
Gallerie Dell'Accademia, Venice

F|OR unto us a child is born, unto us a son is given: and the government shall be upon his shoulder:

ISAIAH 9·6

Antonio Correggio (c. 1489-1534)
The Virgin Adoring the Child Jesus
Uffizi, Florence

AND his name shall be called Wonderful, Counsellor, The mighty God, The everlasting Father, The Prince of Peace.

ISAIAH 9·6

Pellegrino Tibaldi (1527-96)
The Adoration of the Child Jesus
Galleria Borghese, Rome

The Worship of the Shepherds

AND there were in the same country shepherds abiding in the field, keeping watch over their flock by night.

And, lo, the angel of the Lord came upon them, and the glory of the Lord shone round about them: and they were sore afraid.

And the angel said unto them, Fear not: for, behold, I bring you good tidings of great joy, which shall be to all people.

For unto you is born this day in the city of David a Saviour, which is Christ the Lord.

LUKE 2·8-11

Antoniazzo Romano (active 1461-1508)
The Nativity (detail)
Metropolitan Museum, New York

AND this shall be a sign unto you; Ye shall find the babe wrapped in swaddling clothes, lying in a manger.

And suddenly there was with the angel a multitude of the heavenly host praising God, and saying,

Glory to God in the highest, and on earth peace, good will toward men.

LUKE 2:12-14

Manuscript page detail (15th century)
The Annunciation of the Shepherds
Osterreichische National Bibliothek,
Vienna (Bridgeman Art Library)

40

AND it came to pass, as the angels were gone away from them into heaven, the shepherds said one to another, Let us now go even unto Bethlehem, and see this thing which is come to pass, which the Lord hath made known unto us.

LUKE 2:15

Nicolaes Berchem (1620-83)
The Annunciation to the Shepherds
City of Bristol Museum & Art Gallery
(Bridgeman Art Library)

AND they came with haste, and found Mary, and Joseph, and the babe lying in a manger.

LUKE 2·16

Giorgio Barbarelli Giorgione (1475-1510)
The Adoration of the Shepherds
National Gallery, Washington

Bonifazio Veronese de Pitati (c. 1487-1553)
The Adoration of the Shepherds (detail)
Prado, Madrid

The Worship of the Magi

Benozzo di Lese Gozzoli (c. 1421-97)
The Journey of the Magi
Palazzo Medici-Riccardi, Florence
(Bridgeman Art Library)

NOW when Jesus was born in Bethlehem of Judaea in the days of Herod the king, behold, there came wise men from the east to Jerusalem,

Saying, Where is he that is born King of the Jews? for we have seen his star in the east, and are come to worship him.

MATTHEW 2:1-2

THEY departed; and lo, the star, which they saw in the east, went before them, till it came and stood over where the young child was.

When they saw the star, they rejoiced with exceeding great joy.

MATTHEW 2:9-10

Beato Angelico (1387-1455)
The Adoration of the Magi
National Gallery, Washington

AND when they were come into the house, they saw the young child with Mary his mother, and fell down, and worshipped him: and when they had opened their treasures, they presented unto him gifts; gold, and frankincense, and myrrh.

MATTHEW 2·11

Pieter Bruegel the Elder (c. 1525-69)
The Adoration of the Kings
National Gallery, London

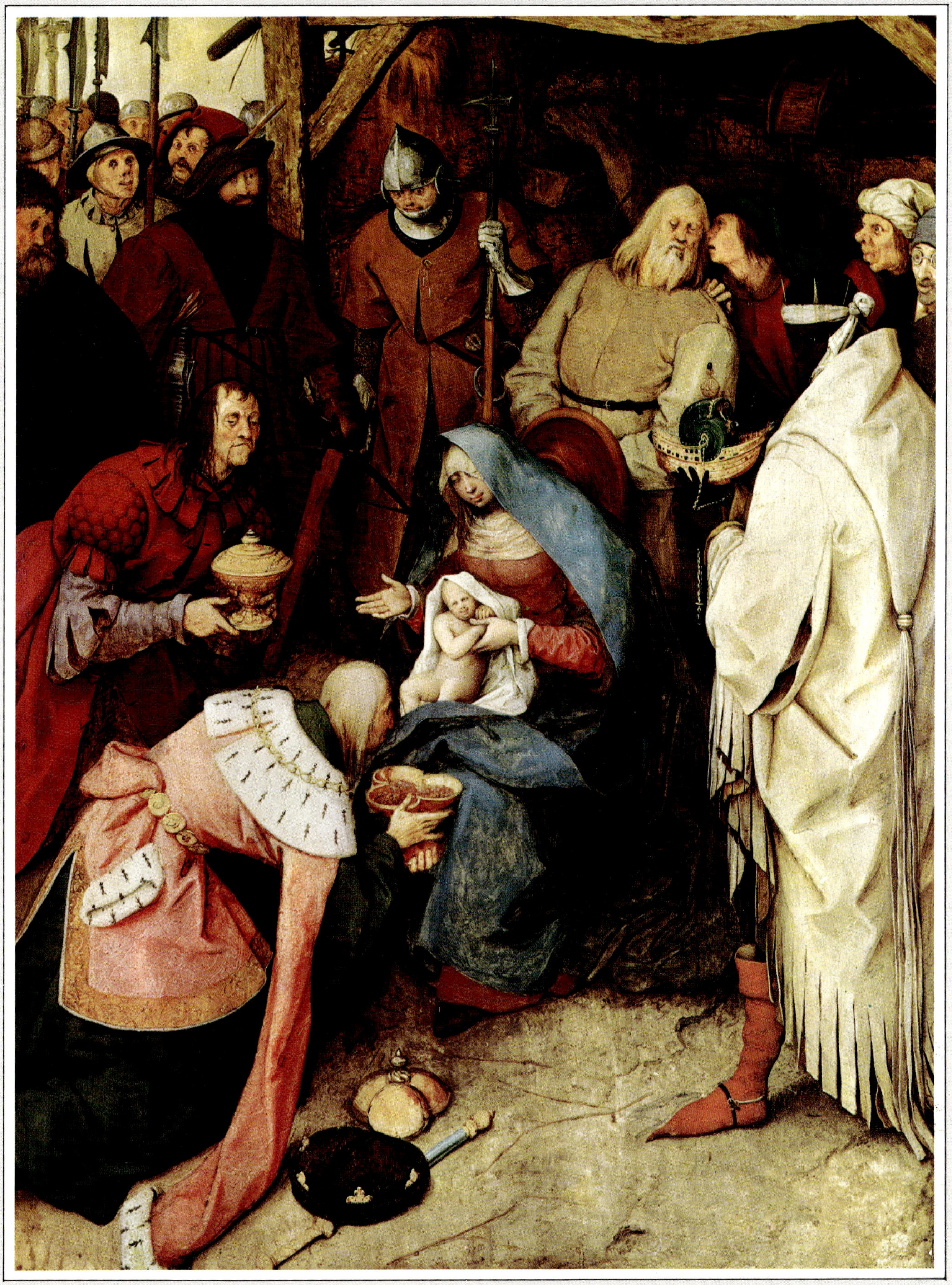

The Presentation

Philippe de Champaigne (1602-74)
The Presentation in the Temple (detail)
Musées Royaux des Beaux-Arts
de Belgique, Brussels

Ambrogio Lorenzetti (active 1319-48)
The Presentation in the Temple
Uffizi, Florence

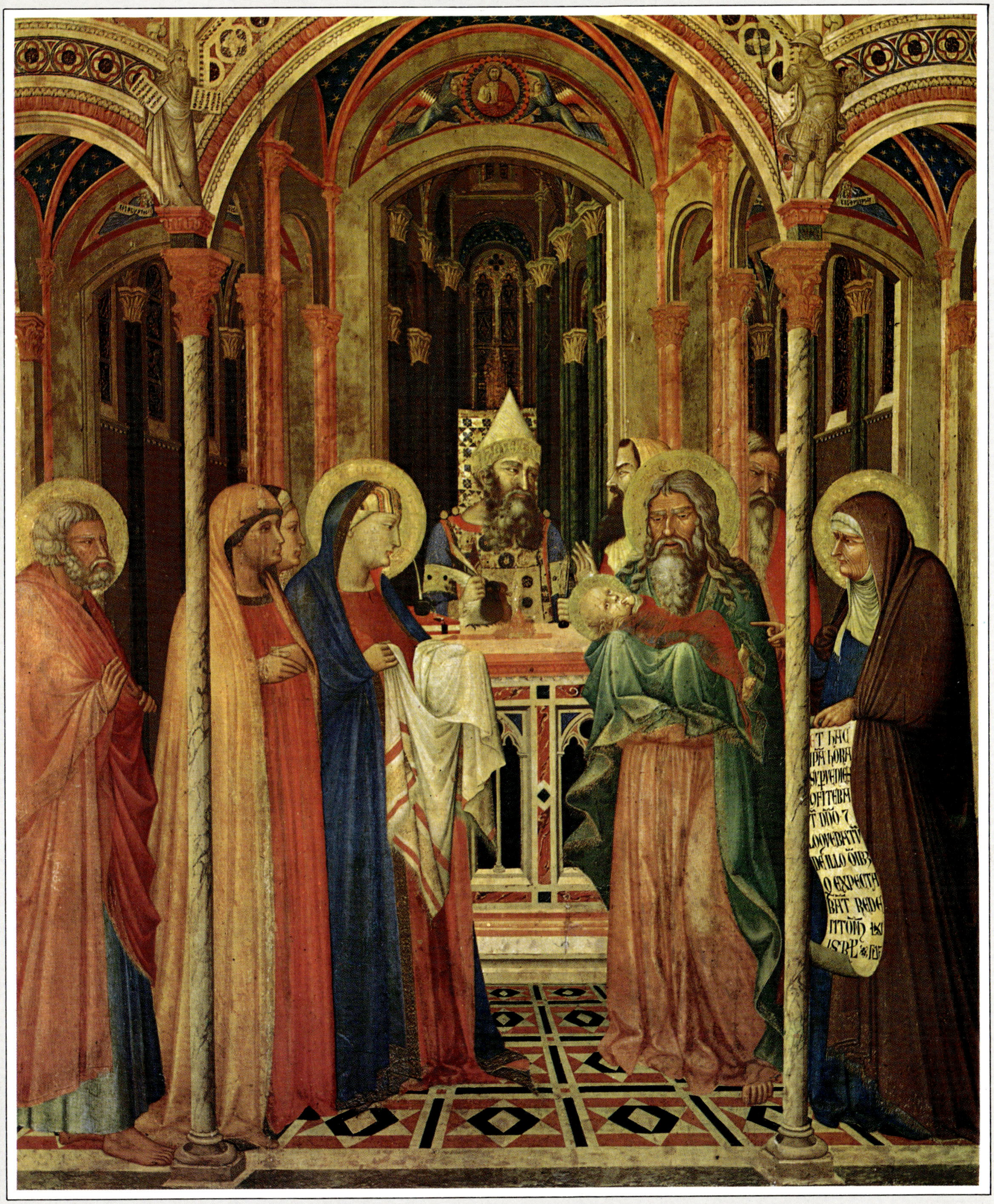

AND when the days of her purification according to the law of Moses were accomplished, they brought him to Jerusalem, to present him to the Lord;

LUKE 2·22

Hans Memling (1430/5-94)
The Presentation of Jesus in the Temple
Prado, Madrid

53

AND, behold, there was a man in Jerusalem, whose name was Simeon; and the same man was just and devout, waiting for the consolation of Israel: and the Holy Ghost was upon him.

And it was revealed unto him by the Holy Ghost, that he should not see death, before he had seen the Lord's Christ.

LUKE 2·25-26

Fra Baccio della Porta Bartolommeo (1472/5-1517)
The Presentation in the Temple
Kunsthistorisches Museum, Vienna

AND he came by the Spirit into the temple and when the parents brought in the child Jesus, to do for him after the custom of the law,

> Then took he him up in his arms, and blessed God.

LUKE 2:27-28

AND Simeon blessed them, and said unto Mary his mother, Behold, this child is set for the fall and rising again of many in Israel; and for a sign which shall be spoken against;

LUKE 2:34

Philippe de Champaigne (1602-74)
The Presentation in the Temple
Musées Royaux des Beaux-Arts de Belgique, Brussels

57

The Flight into Egypt

Antonio Correggio (c. 1489-1534)
Resting in Egypt (detail)
Uffizi, Florence

Domenico Feti (c. 1589-1624)
The Flight into Egypt
Kunsthistorisches Museum, Vienna

Gerard David (d. 1523)
The Rest on the Flight into Egypt
National Gallery, Washington

BEHOLD, the angel of the Lord appeareth to Joseph in a dream, saying, Arise, and take the young child and his mother, and flee into Egypt, and be thou there until I bring thee word: for Herod will seek the young child to destroy him.

When he arose, he took the young child and his mother by night, and departed into Egypt:

MATTHEW 2·13-14

AND was there until the death of Herod: that it might be fulfilled which was spoken of the Lord by the prophet, saying, Out of Egypt have I called my son.

MATTHEW 2:15

Antonio Correggio (c. 1489-1534)
Resting in Egypt
Uffizi, Florence